UTILIZING THE CREDIT CARD

HOW A CREDIT CARD CAN HELP YOU ACHIEVE A LASER FOCUS ON YOUR GOALS

KATE .P

Contents

CHAPTER ONE

INTRODUCTION

In the ever-changing world of personal finance, people are always looking for practical ways to maximize their wealth. Of all the tools at one's disposal, credit cards are particularly useful because they are adaptable and may be utilized wisely to provide a number of advantages in addition to making transactions easier. Using credit cards wisely can help you achieve financial goals, career objectives, or personal aspirations by providing laser focus. This is in addition to being simply convenient.

We explore how credit cards may be very useful companions in your quest for success in this exploration. From using reward systems to developing frugal spending practices, we reveal the ways in which these seemingly insignificant bits of plastic can become invaluable tools in your pursuit of success.

We will also explore the psychology of credit card use, illuminating how these instruments affect our purchasing patterns and mold our attitudes toward money. Understanding the nuances of credit card dynamics can help you take advantage of their potential to support your objectives and guide your financial path toward more clarity and direction.

Come along on this adventure to uncover the credit card's transformational power and learn how they may steadily advance you toward your goals. Whether your goals are to accumulate income, follow your passions, or find personal fulfillment, the knowledge presented in this talk will enable you to use credit cards as tools of concentration, allowing you to move toward success with direction and clarity.

Setting Goals and Its Power in Personal Finance

Setting goals is an effective way for people to prioritize their spending and saving, define their goals clearly, and maintain motivation to reach their financial goals. Goal-setting can have a big influence in the following ways:

Clarity and Focus: Having well-defined financial objectives aids people in identifying their financial objectives. Whether the aim is home ownership, debt repayment, retirement savings, or a dream vacation, having well-defined objectives gives focus and direction.

Motivation: Setting and achieving goals can be quite effective. People are more likely to maintain discipline in their financial habits and make the required sacrifices to accomplish their goals when they have specific aims to aim for.

Setting priorities: Not all monetary objectives are of the same importance. Setting goals enables people to order their priorities according to their values and long-term goals. By doing this, they can spend their money wisely and prevent spending it on items that aren't important to them.

Measurable Progress: Establishing precise, quantifiable objectives enables people to monitor their development over time. This sense of accomplishment has the power to inspire people greatly and keep them on course even in the face of obstacles or disappointments.

Accountability: You can develop a sense of accountability by discussing your goals with friends, family, and financial experts. People are more likely to remain devoted to and responsible for their financial decisions when they are aware that others are aware of their objectives.

Adaptability: As priorities or circumstances change over time, financial goals may also need to be modified. Setting and revising goals on a regular basis enables people to adjust to changing circumstances and stay on track to accomplish their goals.

Financial Discipline: A person's ability to create and uphold sound financial practices, such as prudent saving, budgeting, and investing, is frequently a prerequisite for setting objectives. These behaviors have the potential to improve resilience and financial discipline over time.

Sense of Achievement: Reaching financial objectives makes one feel satisfied and accomplished. Reaching financial objectives, such as debt repayment, savings milestones, or long-term investment targets, can increase self-assurance and self-worth.

Setting goals is a crucial component of personal finance that can empower people to take charge of their financial destiny, maintain motivation, and eventually realize their ambitions. People can create a strong basis for their financial success and well-being by committing to and setting quantifiable, well-defined goals.

Comprehending Credit Cards

It's essential to comprehend credit cards in order to properly manage personal money. Here are important things to think about:

A credit card: what is it?A credit card is a plastic payment card that is issued by a financial institution. The cardholder agrees to repay the borrowed amount plus any associated fees and interest in order to use the credit card to make transactions.

Credit limit: The maximum sum of money that a credit card user is authorized to borrow is known as the credit limit. The credit card issuer makes this determination based on various variables, including the cardholder's income and creditworthiness.

Interest rates: If an outstanding balance is not paid off by the due date, an annual percentage rate, or APR, is usually applied. It is crucial to comprehend the annual percentage rate (APR), promotional offers, introductory rates, and the consequences of missing payments or going over credit limit.

Minimum payment: In order to avoid late fees and penalties, cardholders must pay the minimum amount stated on their credit card statements before the deadline. Paying just the minimum, however, may result in exorbitant interest costs and increase the amount of time needed to pay off the debt.

Grace period: Many credit cards come with a grace period, usually lasting between 21 and 25 days, during which time new purchases are exempt from interest charges if the entire balance is paid off before the due date. Cardholders that are aware of the grace period can prevent unwarranted interest charges.

costs: There are several types of costs that can be associated with credit cards, including annual, late, balance transfer, cash advance, and foreign transaction fees. It's critical to understand these costs and account for them when calculating how much using the credit card will cost.

Impact on credit score: A person's credit score can be greatly impacted by their use of credit cards, as well as by their payment history, credit utilization ratio, and length of credit history. A strong credit score can be improved or maintained by using credit cards responsibly, which includes paying your bills on time and keeping your balances low compared to your credit limit.

Benefits and rewards: A lot of credit cards come with extended warranties, cashback incentives, travel insurance, and purchase protection, among other benefits. Cardholders may get the most out of their credit cards by being aware of these perks and rewards.

Security: Built-in security features on credit cards include fraud prevention and no liability for unapproved charges. It is imperative to take security measures to safeguard credit card information, like making online transactions on secure websites and routinely checking account activity for any unusual expenditures.

All things considered, being aware of the rules, benefits, and possible risks associated with credit cards enables people to use credit responsibly and manage their money more skillfully.

Fundamentals of Credit Card Features

Anyone thinking about getting a credit card has to know the fundamentals of how they work. This is an explanation:

Credit Line: The credit card issuer grants you a specific credit limit when you apply for one. This is the most money you are able to borrow with the card. Your income, other financial responsibilities, and credit history are some of the elements that go into determining your credit limit.

Making Purchases: You can use a credit card to make both in-person and online purchases at a variety of retailers. The money is essentially borrowed from the credit card provider when you make a transaction and charge it to your credit card.

Billing Cycle: Credit card transactions are generally categorized into monthly billing cycles. You are able to make purchases during this time up to your credit limit. The credit card issuer sends you a statement at the end of each billing cycle that lists all of your transactions along with the balance you owe.

CHAPTER TWO

Minimum Payment: The amount that must be paid by the deadline in order to maintain the good standing of your account will be indicated on your credit card statement as the minimum payment. Usually between one and three percent of your entire balance, plus any applicable interest and fees, is the minimum payment amount.

Interest Charges: Should you fail to pay off your entire balance by the deadline, interest will be charged on the amount that remains outstanding and will be carried over to the following billing cycle. The interest rate is applied to the outstanding balance and is referred to as the Annual Percentage Rate (APR).

Grace Period: Some credit cards come with a grace period, often lasting between 21 and 25 days, during which you can pay off your debt in full by the due date and avoid paying interest on any new purchases. It is important to review the terms and conditions of your credit card because not all credit cards include a grace period.

costs: There are a number of different types of costs that credit cards may have, such as annual, late, balance transfer, cash advance, and foreign transaction fees. It's important to comprehend these costs and how your card usage is affected by them.

Impact on Credit Score: A number of factors, such as the length of your credit history, credit utilization ratio, and payment history, are related to your credit score. Your credit score can be improved by using credit cards responsibly, which includes paying your bills on time and maintaining low balances compared to your credit limit.

You may utilize credit cards responsibly, prevent needless fees and interest charges, and establish a good credit history by being aware of these fundamental features.

Credit Card Types and Their Characteristics

There are several varieties of credit cards, each with unique features and advantages designed to meet the needs and preferences of the consumer. The following are some typical credit card kinds and their characteristics:

Basic credit cards with conventional features like fees, interest rates, and credit limits are known as standard credit cards. While they might not provide rewards or exclusive advantages, they do offer a practical means of making transactions and establishing credit.

Credit Cards with Rewards: Credit cards with rewards give users incentives to spend by matching every dollar they spend with cash back, points, or miles. You can exchange these rewards for gift cards, goods, travel, and statement credits. Rewards cards come in various subtypes, such as:

With cashback credit cards, you can receive cash rewards equal to a percentage of your purchases.

Travel rewards credit cards allow you to accrue points or miles that can be used to pay for lodging, transportation, and other travel-related costs.

Credit cards with points: Collect points that can be exchanged for merchandise, gift cards, or travel.

Airline and Hotel Credit Cards: These cards are co-branded with particular airline or hotel companies and come with benefits like elite status, priority boarding, free checked bags, bonus miles or points for transactions made with the associated airline or hotel, and free hotel stays or upgrades.

Credit Cards with Cashback: These credit cards return a portion of your purchases to you in the form of cash. For various spending categories, including groceries, gas, dining out, or general shopping, they could have varied cashback rates.

Credit Cards with Security Deposits: Credit cards with security deposits normally have a credit limit. These cards can assist people in establishing or repairing credit because they are intended for those with a limited or damaged credit history. Over time, your credit score may rise as a result of using a secured credit card responsibly.

Student Credit Cards: College students with little or no credit history are the target market for these credit cards. They frequently provide low credit limits, incentives for high grades, and instructional materials to teach kids how to use credit cards responsibly.

Credit cards with balance transfers: These cards let you move amounts from other high-interest credit cards to the new one, frequently with a promotional rate that is low or 0% APR for a set amount of time. By doing this, you can reduce interest costs and accelerate the repayment of current debt.

Business Credit Cards: Designed with small business owners in mind, business credit cards come with features like employee cards with spending limitations, tools for managing expenses, incentives on business-related purchases, and business-specific benefits like travel or office supply discounts.

To select the credit card that best suits your spending preferences and financial needs, it's critical to thoroughly analyze the features, perks, costs, and conditions of several options. In addition, you may optimize the advantages of your selected credit card and establish a good credit history by using credit cards responsibly, which includes paying off your debt in full each month and avoiding pointless fees.

Establishing Budgetary Objectives

A key to reaching financial success and stability is setting financial goals. Here's a how-to guide for creating sensible financial objectives:

Assess Your present Financial Situation: Evaluate your present financial status before establishing any goals. Determine your earnings, outlays, possessions, liabilities, investments, and savings. Knowing where you stand financially can enable you to make reasonable and doable goals.

Establish Your Goals: Make sure you know exactly what you hope to accomplish financially.

You can set medium-term (1–5 years), long-term (5+ years), or short-term (achievable within a year) goals. Typical financial objectives consist of:

Debt repayment

accumulating an emergency reserve

Putting money aside for retirement

Purchasing a house

Putting money aside for a trip

Putting money into investments to build wealth

financing your own or your kids' education

Set SMART (specific, measurable, attainable, relevant, and time-bound) goals for yourself:

Specific: Clearly state your goals and objectives. Saying "I want to save money" is not as specific as saying "I want to save $5,000 for a down payment on a home."

Measurable: Establish specific benchmarks to gauge your development. Establish the amount and timeline of the money you need to save.

Achievable: Ensure that your objectives are reasonable in light of your available funds, time, and resources. Steer clear of establishing too ambitious or unreachable goals.

Relevant: Make sure your objectives line up with your priorities, values, and long-term dreams.

Time-Bound: Establish due dates for accomplishing your objectives to foster accountability and a sense of urgency.

Set Priorities for Your Goals: Not every goal has the same importance. Prioritize your goals based on which are most important or urgent for you. It could be necessary for you to focus on high-priority goals before addressing others.

Divide Your Objectives Into Doable Steps: Divide each objective into more doable tasks or benchmarks. Your ambitions will become less daunting and more achievable as a result. Make a schedule and an action plan to ensure that every step is completed.

Track Your Progress: Keep tabs on your financial objectives and evaluate them on a regular basis. Evaluate what's working well and any areas that might require modifications. Reward yourself for small victories along the road to keep your motivation up.

Remain Adaptive and Flexible: Things might change in life, so be ready to modify your plans as necessary. Maintain your adaptability and flexibility while staying true to your major financial goals.

Seek Professional Advice if Needed: You should think about speaking with a financial advisor if you need help with complicated financial concerns or if you're confused how to create financial goals. They may offer you individualized advice and assist in creating a thorough financial strategy that is catered to your requirements and objectives.

You may take charge of your finances and work toward realizing your goals by prioritizing your goals, breaking them down into manageable steps, making SMART financial goals, and keeping track of your progress.

Making Use of Rewards Programs for Credit Cards

Utilizing credit card rewards programs is a great method to get the most out of your credit cards. This is a how-to guide for making the most of credit card rewards programs:

Recognize Your Rewards Program: Learn about the rewards program that your credit card company offers. Know how to accrue rewards, what kinds of rewards are available (miles, points, and cash back), and how to use them.

Pick the Correct Credit Card: Make sure the benefits on your credit card match your spending preferences and way of life. For instance, a cashback card can be better for regular purchases, but a travel rewards card might be more advantageous if you travel regularly.

Maximize Bonus Categories: A lot of credit cards come with bonus benefits for certain categories of expenditure, such travel, entertainment, dining out, grocery, and gas. Utilize your card whenever you can to make purchases in these categories to take advantage of these bonus categories.

Meet Sign-Up Bonuses: Within the first few months of opening an account, new cardholders who meet specific spending conditions are frequently eligible for sign-up bonuses on credit cards. To maximize these advantages, plan your purchases such that they will reach the expenditure requirement.

Prevent Interest Charges: It's crucial to pay off the entire balance on your credit card each month to prevent interest from building up in order to get the most out of your rewards program. Interest expenses have the ability to swiftly offset the worth of any gains made.

Redeem Wisely: Examine the different ways you can redeem points from your rewards program, including gift cards, products, statement credits, airline reservations, and transfers to other loyalty programs. Pick redemption strategies that maximize the value of your awards.

Track Offers and Promotions: Keep a watch out for any time-limited sales, promotions, or special offers from your credit card company. These could be further incentives, savings, or other benefits that raise the worth of your rewards program.

Combine and Pool Points: You may want to think about consolidating your points or miles into a single account if you have many credit cards from the same issuer that provide rewards programs. This can open more redemption choices and facilitate reward management.

Make Use of Online Portals and Shopping Portals: A number of credit card companies provide online shopping portals or retail partnerships, allowing you to accrue extra benefits for purchases made on these platforms. Utilize these chances to increase the benefits you receive for your purchases.

Stay Organized: To make sure you're getting the most out of your rewards program, keep track of your balances, expiration dates, and redemption possibilities. To efficiently manage your incentives, think about utilizing a spreadsheet or a mobile app.

You may maximize your credit card usage and benefit from earned rewards by comprehending how credit card rewards programs operate and putting these tactics into practice. Just keep in mind to handle credit sensibly and refrain from going overboard when pursuing rewards.

Setting and Monitoring Expenses

Creating a budget and keeping track of spending are essential tools for successful personal money management. Here's a how-to for making a budget and keeping track of your spending:

Calculate Your Income: To begin, figure out how much money you make each month from all sources, including wages, salaries, bonuses, freelancing, rental income, and other sources.

Enumerate All of Your Fixed Expenses: A fixed expense is one that is paid for on a monthly basis and is a recurrent expense. This covers utility bills, insurance premiums, loan payments, rent or mortgage payments, and subscription services.

Determine Variable Expenses: Variable expenses are those that change every month according on consumption or usage. Food, eating out, entertainment, travel, clothes, and personal hygiene products are a few examples.

Establish Financial Goals: Decide on your short- and long-term financial objectives, such as debt repayment, emergency fund accumulation, vacation savings, and retirement investment. In your budget, set aside a certain percentage of your money for these objectives.

Create Spending Categories: Arrange your costs according to their type and importance. Housing, transportation, groceries, utilities, healthcare, savings, debt payback, entertainment, and other sporadic costs are examples of common categories.

Allocate Funds: Based on your income, costs, and financial objectives, allocate a certain sum of money to each spending area. Prioritize your most important spending while still making space for extracurriculars. Be sensible.

Monitor Your Expenses: Keep a note of each item you buy and transaction you make. Pen and paper, spreadsheets, budgeting software, and internet banking tools are just a few of the tools at your disposal. Accurately classify your spending to learn more about your spending patterns.

Evaluate and Make Adjustments Often: Try to review your spending and budget once a month at the latest. Examine any differences between your actual and planned spending to see if you are overspending in any areas. Make necessary adjustments to your budget to stay on course and meet your financial objectives.

Eliminate Needless Expenses: Seek ways to cut back on discretionary spending and eliminate needless expenses. Find places where you can cut expenses without compromising your financial security or standard of living.

Create an Emergency Fund: Set aside money on a regular basis to pay for unforeseen costs or financial difficulties. Try to have an emergency fund in a different savings account that is equal to three to six months' worth of living expenses.

Seek Accountability and Support: Talk to a trustworthy friend, relative, or financial expert about your budgeting objectives and progress. Having support and accountability from someone helps keep you motivated and dedicated to your budgeting endeavors.

You may take charge of your finances, reach your financial objectives, and move toward financial stability and success by making a budget, keeping track of your spending, and routinely assessing your financial status.

Taking Care of Credit Card Debt

Maintaining good financial standing and averting long-term financial difficulties require effective credit card debt management. The following actions will assist you in efficiently handling your credit card debt:

Evaluate Your Debt: To begin, get all of your credit card bills and determine your overall debt. Make a note of the due dates, minimum monthly payments, interest rates, and balances on each credit card.

Make a Budget: Come up with a plan that details your monthly spending, debt repayment, and income. Set aside a percentage of your income to pay off credit card debt in addition to preserving money for future purchases and necessary bills.

Set High-Interest Debt as a Priority: Make it a point to pay off credit cards with the highest interest rates initially. You can reduce interest costs and accelerate debt repayment by giving high-intcrest debt priority.

Pay More Than the Minimum: When it's feasible, pay your credit cards' monthly minimum amount. Paying just the minimum amount will increase the total interest paid over time and lengthen the time it takes to pay off your debt.

Employ a Debt Repayment Plan: To expedite your debt payoff, think about utilizing a debt repayment plan, such as the debt avalanche or debt snowball approach. Paying off debts with the highest interest rates first is the goal of the debt avalanche strategy. Regardless of interest rates, the debt snowball strategy focuses on paying off the lowest bills first in order to build momentum and motivation.

Consolidate Debt: Look into possibilities for reducing your debt, like combining several loans into one or moving high-interest credit card balances to a new card with a cheaper interest rate. When considering consolidation options, pay attention to any debt transfer fees, introductory rates, and repayment periods.

Engage in Creditor Negotiation: Speak with your creditors to work out better terms for repayment, such as lowered interest rates or fees. Many creditors are open to collaborating with you to come up with a win-win plan for paying off your debt.

Avoid Taking on More Debt: While you're trying to pay off your current debt, resist the urge to take on additional credit card debt. Remain mindful of living within your means and refrain from utilizing credit cards for impulsive expenditures.

Seek Professional Help if Needed: If you're finding it difficult to handle your credit card debt on your own, you might want to think about getting in touch with a financial advisor or credit counselor. If you need it, they can offer you individualized guidance, help with budgeting and debt repayment plans, and support as you look into debt relief alternatives.

Remain Patient and Committed: It takes patience, discipline, and time to manage credit card debt. Track your progress, remain dedicated to your debt payback strategy, and acknowledge minor accomplishments along the way. You may become financially independent and pay off your credit card debt with persistence and devotion.

It's important to keep in mind that controlling credit card debt is a gradual process, so you must exercise patience and perseverance. You may recover control over your finances and lay the groundwork for a better financial future by acting now to pay off debt and strengthen your financial habits.

Making Use of Promotions and Initial Offers

Making the most of opening deals and promotions can be a calculated move when it comes to banking, credit cards, and other financial items. The following are some tips for maximizing initial offers:

Examine and Compare deals: Investigate the various deals on the market before submitting an application for a credit card or creating a new account. Find the initial deals that best fit your financial needs and objectives by comparing offers like sign-up bonuses, 0% APR periods, cashback incentives, or waived fees.

Study the Terms and Conditions: Pay close attention to the terms and conditions to grasp the specifics of the introductory offer, such as the length of the promotional period, the eligibility requirements, and any possible costs or limitations. Verify that you are aware of all the requirements necessary to accept the offer, including any conditions or restrictions.

Benefit from Sign-Up Bonuses: A lot of credit cards provide sign-up bonuses to new users who fulfill certain spending targets in the first several months of opening an account. Make thoughtful purchase plans to reach the spending requirement and be eligible for the bonus in order to optimize sign-up bonuses.

CHAPTER THREE

Use 0% APR Periods: For a set number of months during the promotional period, certain credit cards offer 0% APR on purchases or debt transfers. Make major purchases or transfer high-interest balances during certain special times to avoid paying interest. But be aware of any debt transfer costs as well as the standard APR that will take effect once the promotional period expires.

Accumulate Reward Points or Cashback: Seek out credit cards that, as part of their introductory offers, provide sizeable rewards or cashback benefits. Use your card for regular purchases and take advantage of bonus categories or promotional spending incentives to make the most out of your points earned.

Meet conditions and Deadlines: In order to be eligible for introductory offers, you must fulfill all eligibility conditions and the issuer's deadlines. This could include fulfilling a spending requirement within a given time limit, triggering the deal, or keeping your account in good standing.

Watch Your Accounts: Make sure you're following the conditions for introductory deals and making the most of the benefits that are available to you by keeping an eye on your spending, balances, and account activity. Make sure to frequently review your account statements for any inconsistencies or problems, and set reminders for crucial dates.

Be Strategic and Responsible: Although introductory offers can yield significant advantages, it is imperative to employ them in a thoughtful and conscientious manner. Refrain from going overboard with purchases or taking on more debt than you can manage, and be aware of any additional costs or fees related to the offer.

You can optimize the advantages of financial products and services, save fees and interest charges, and obtain worthwhile rewards or incentives to help you achieve your financial objectives by skillfully utilizing introductory offers and promotions.

To ensure a steady and secure financial future, you must safeguard your credit and financial well-being. The following are crucial actions to protect your finances and credit:

Keep an Eye on Your Credit Report: Obtain a copy of your credit report on a regular basis from each of the three major credit agencies (TransUnion, Equifax, and Experian) and look for any mistakes or indications of identity theft. Every 12 months, you can obtain a free credit report from each bureau by visiting AnnualCreditReport.com.

Protect Your Personal Information: Use caution while disclosing any sensitive personal information, especially over the phone or online, such as your bank account information, passwords, or Social Security number. When transacting online, make sure you use secure websites and refrain from answering queries for personal or financial information that are not requested.

Boost Security and Passwords: For an extra degree of protection, use two-factor authentication in addition to creating strong, one-of-a-kind passwords for all of your online accounts. Update your hardware, operating system, and security software to guard against viruses, malware, and other online dangers.

Keep an eye on Account Activity: Continually check your credit card and bank statements for any unusual or questionable charges. To stop more harm, notify your financial institutions right away of any inconsistencies or fraudulent activities.

Establish Fraud Alerts and Credit Freezes: To help stop illegal access to your credit information, think about putting fraud alerts or credit freezes on your credit reports. Credit freezes completely prevent access to your credit record, while fraud warnings urge creditors to take additional measures to confirm your identity before opening new accounts.

Be Aware of Scams: Be on the lookout for popular scams such phishing emails, phony lottery or sweepstakes offers, scams posing as the IRS, and investment deceptions. Avert sending personal or financial information to unidentified or unreliable sources, and exercise caution when responding to unsolicited communications or offers that appear too good to be true.

Handle Debt Responsibly: To keep your credit score high, pay your payments on time, refrain from using all of your credit cards, and keep your credit utilization ratio low. If you're having trouble paying off debt, get in touch with your lenders or think about seeking help from a respectable credit counseling organization.

Keep Yourself Educated and Informed: Remain up to date on the newest frauds, trends, and safe practices for safeguarding your finances and credit. Keep abreast of any modifications to financial legislation, keep an eye on news sources for information on security incidents or data breaches, and ask reliable people for assistance if you have any questions or concerns.

You may lower your chance of identity theft, fraud, and financial difficulty by taking proactive measures to protect your credit and financial well-being. You'll also feel more at ease knowing that your finances are safe.

Selecting the Best Credit Card for Your Objectives

Selecting the best credit card for your needs requires taking into account a number of variables, including your spending patterns, financial goals, way of life, and preferences. This is a step-by-step guide to assist you in choosing the credit card that best suits your needs:

Establish Your Objectives: Choose the things you hope to accomplish with your credit card. Are you hoping to obtain incentives, establish credit, reduce interest costs, or profit from particular advantages or benefits? Your card picking process will be guided by the clarity of your aims.

Recognize Your Spending Patterns: Determine where you spend the most money by examining your spending habits. Think about categories like travel, entertainment, petrol, groceries, eating, and regular costs. Select a credit card that provides advantages or rewards that correspond with your main areas of spending.

Think About Rewards and Benefits: Compare and contrast the various credit cards' rewards plans and perks. Cashback, points, miles, and statement credits are examples of common rewards. Seek out credit cards with rewards programs that are significant, bonuses for signing up, and redemption possibilities that fit your needs.

Evaluate costs and Costs: Examine the yearly, international transaction, balance transfer, and late payment costs that are attached to each credit card. Assess whether owning the card will result in more perks and incentives than it will cost, particularly if there is an annual fee.

Examine Interest Rates and APR: If you intend to carry a balance on your credit card, be sure to compare the interest rates and Annual Percentage Rates (APR) of various credit cards. Consider promotional deals, such as 0% APR periods for purchases or balance transfers, and select a card with a competitive annual percentage rate.

Examine Introductory deals: To get the most out of your credit card, take advantage of introductory deals like sign-up bonuses, 0% APR periods, or waived fees. Think about how lengthy the introductory period is and if it fits in with your immediate financial objectives.

Examine Extra Features: Credit cards offer a number of extra features and benefits, so go beyond rewards and fees. These could include free upgrades, extended warranties, concierge services, purchase protection, travel insurance, and access to airport lounges.

Examine Eligibility and Approval Odds: When selecting a credit card, take your financial profile and credit score into account. While some cards are more accessible to people with medium or fair credit, others may demand great credit. To determine your chances of being approved, use pre-qualification resources or credit card comparison websites.

Read Reviews and Research: To learn more about cardholder experiences, the caliber of customer service, and general satisfaction, do some internet research on credit card possibilities and read reviews from reliable sources. To make an informed choice, consider both positive and negative input.

Apply for the Card: After you've decided which credit card best suits your needs, apply online or via the issuer's website. Fill out your application completely, and be ready to provide proof of identity and income if needed.

Through careful consideration of these variables and adherence to a methodical process, you can select a credit card that complements your objectives, way of life, and budgetary inclinations, and optimize the advantages and incentives associated with your card utilization.

Automating Account Management and Payment Processes

One practical and efficient strategy to manage your finances and reduce the likelihood of missing payments and late fees is to automate account administration and payment processing. Here's how to effectively manage your accounts and schedule payments:

Establish Automatic Bill Payments: A lot of banks and other financial organizations have online bill payment systems that let you plan regular payments for expenses like utilities, rent or mortgage, loans, insurance premiums, and other obligations. To guarantee that these recurrent costs are paid on time each month, set up automated payments.

CHAPTER FOUR

Plan Credit Card Payments: To set up automatic payments for your credit card bills, visit the websites of your credit card issuer or your bank's online bill pay service. Each month, you have the option of paying the entire statement balance, the minimum amount owed, or a customized amount. To make sure there are enough cash, choose a payment date that coincides with your pay plan.

Enroll in Auto-Pay for Debts and Loans: If you have debts or loans, such as personal, auto, or school loans, you should think about signing up for the auto-pay services that lenders offer. By automatically deducting your monthly payment from your bank account, auto-payments lower your chance of missing or being late with payments and can even make you eligible for interest rate savings.

Automate Savings Contributions: To automate your savings contributions, set up automatic transfers from your checking account to your investment or savings accounts. Choose a monthly savings goal, either a set amount or a percentage of your salary, and plan your transfers appropriately. This aids in steadily increasing your savings over time.

Use Alerts and Reminders: Keep track of account activity, impending payments, low balances, and other crucial notifications by making use of the account alerts and reminders provided by your bank or other financial organizations. To get timely reminders and updates, set up email, text message, or push notification alerts.

Handle Budgets and Track Spending: To keep tabs on your spending, classify transactions, and keep an eye on your budget in real time, use apps or software that help with budgeting. To make managing your finances easier, a lot of budgeting applications let you link your credit cards and bank accounts so that transactions are automatically imported and spending are categorized.

Review and Adjust Often: To make sure everything is operating as it should, check your account balances, spending trends, and automated payments on a regular basis. If your income, expenses, or financial objectives change, you should modify your automated payments or savings contributions.

Keep an Eye Out for Unauthorized Transactions: Even with automation, it's important to keep an eye out for any unusual or suspicious transactions occurring in your accounts. Examine your credit card and bank statements, and notify your financial institutions right away of any inconsistencies or fraudulent activity.

Update Information as Needed: To guarantee smooth account management, keep your contact information, payment methods, and account information current. If you alter your contact details, apply for a new credit card, or move banks, you must update your payment information.

You can simplify your financial tasks, lower your chance of missing payments or incurring late penalties, and maintain organization and control over your funds with little effort by automating payments and account management.

Monitoring Development and Modifying Approaches

Effective personal financial management requires monitoring results and making necessary strategy adjustments. Here's how to keep an eye on your financial development and modify your plans as needed:

Set clear, Measurable Financial Goals: To effectively monitor your progress, set clear, measurable financial goals. Whether your goal is debt repayment, retirement savings, or emergency fund accumulation, having specific goals will keep you motivated and focused.

Review Your Finances Frequently: Allocate time on a regular basis, perhaps once a month or once every three months, to examine your financial status. Analyze your earnings, outlays, investments, debt, savings, and progress toward your objectives. Make any necessary modifications after using this review to pinpoint areas that need work.

Track Spending and Budgets: To make sure you're remaining within your financial boundaries, keep an eye on your spending patterns and periodically check your budget. To classify spending, examine patterns, and pinpoint areas where you can make savings or reallocate money to your objectives, use budgeting tools or software.

Keep an eye on Debt Reduction: If you're making debt payments, keep tabs on your progress by keeping an eye on your interest rates, outstanding balances, and payment history. To estimate how long it will take to pay off your debt, use debt payback calculators. You can also look at ways to reduce your debt faster, including the avalanche or snowball methods.

Examine Investment Performance: Pay attention to how your investments such as savings, brokerage, or retirement accounts are performing. Keep an eye on fees, asset allocation, and investment performance. You should also think about periodically rebalancing your portfolio to make sure it fits your financial objectives and risk tolerance.

Check Credit Reports: To ensure accuracy and spot any mistakes or inconsistencies, periodically check your credit reports from the three main credit bureaus. By keeping an eye on your credit report, you can identify fraud or identity theft early on and take the necessary precautions to preserve your credit score.

Modify Plans as Needed: Remain adaptable and prepared to modify your financial plans in response to shifts in your priorities, situation, or outside variables. You should review and make any required adjustments to your budget, savings plan, or investing strategy if you experience unforeseen expenses, changes in income, or changes in your financial goals.

Celebrate Milestones: To keep yourself inspired and motivated, acknowledge and celebrate your financial successes along the way. Acknowledge your accomplishments and use them as inspiration to keep working toward your financial objectives, whether they are credit card payoffs, savings targets, or portfolio milestones.

Seek Professional Advice: You should think about consulting a financial counselor or planner if you're unclear about how to monitor your success or modify your financial plans. A professional may offer you individualized advice, assist you in evaluating your financial status, and help you create a strategy that will help you accomplish your objectives.

You may stay on track to reaching your financial objectives and lay the groundwork for long-term financial success by routinely monitoring your progress, assessing your finances, and making necessary adjustments to your strategy.

Summary

In conclusion, when used wisely, credit cards may be an effective tool for helping you stay laser-focused on your financial objectives. You can improve your progress towards accomplishing your goals and match your spending habits with them by skillfully utilizing the features and advantages of credit cards.

First of all, credit cards come with a variety of rewards programs that you can customize to fit your unique objectives, such as cash back, points, or miles. Choosing a credit card with benefits that align with your objectives might help you achieve your goals more quickly, whether they involve investing, traveling, or saving money.

Furthermore, a lot of credit cards include promotional offers and introductory deals, including sign-up bonuses or 0% APR periods, which can offer instant rewards and cost savings to help you reach your objectives. With the assistance of these incentives, you can get a head start on your financial path and move closer to your goals right away.

Additionally, credit cards give you flexibility and ease in handling your money by making it simple to track expenses, automate payments, and keep tabs on your progress. You can stay on track to reach your goals and keep an accurate picture of your financial status by using online account management, alert setup, and budgeting tools.

To avoid problems like overspending, racking up high-interest debt, or harming your credit score, you must practice self-control and proper credit card use. You can maximize credit card benefits while minimizing potential negatives by sticking to a budget, making monthly payments in full, and being alert to potential hazards.

All things considered, a credit card can be a useful ally on your path to financial success by giving you the tools to simplify purchases, accrue incentives, and maintain focus on your objectives. You can develop a laser-like concentration on your goals and create the path towards a better financial future by strategically utilizing its capabilities and incorporating it into an all-encompassing financial strategy.

THE END

www.ingramcontent.com/pod-product-compliance
Lightning Source LLC
Chambersburg PA
CBHW070041260726
48658CB00002B/680